Also by Tim Miller:

To the House of the Sun

Hymns & Lamentations

Tim Miller

✣S4N Books

Hymns & Lamentations, by Tim Miller
© 2011 Tim Miller

ISBN 10: 0-9798707-2-0
ISBN 13: 978-0-9798707-2-9

Library of Congress Control Number: 2010914061

Cover Photo by Jenny Miller

✡S4N BOOKS

author's website: www.wordandsilence.com
email: s4nbooks@outlook.com

LAMENTATIONS

1. A lamentation over a man of God 3
2. A lamentation over a community 4
3. A lamentation over a daughter 5
4. A lamentation over a child 6
5. A lamentation over a mother 7
6. A lamentation over many women 8
7. A lamentation over a man 9
8. A lamentation over a man 10
9. A lamentation over a man 11
10. A lamentation over an elderly man 12
11. A lamentation over an elderly man 13
12. A lamentation over a man 14
13. A lamentation over a young woman 15
14. A lamentation over a woman 16
15. A lamentation over a young woman 17
16. A lamentation over a man 18
17. A lamentation over a young woman 19
18. A lamentation over a young woman 20
19. A lamentation over a daughter, wife, & mother 21
20. A lamentation over a woman 22
21. A lamentation over a witness 23
22. A lamentation over two men 24
23. A lamentation over a young man..25
24. A lamentation over a community 26
25. A lamentation over a mother 27
26. A lamentation over a enslaved man 28
27. A lamentation over a community 29
28. A lamentation over a community 30
29. A lamentation over a hanged man.. 31
30. A lamentation over those in mines....................................... 32
31. A lamentation over a slave ship 33

32. A lamentation over a slave ship 34
33. A lamentation over a slave ship 35
34. A lamentation over a slave 36
35. A lamentation over fathers, husbands, & brothers 37
36. A lamentation over a slave 38
37. A lamentation over a slave ship 39
38. A lamentation over a family 40
39. A lamentation over a widow 41
40. A lamentation over the hands, legs, & heart 42
41. A lamentation over the eyes, ears and skin 43
42. A lamentation over the mind, soul, & life 44
43. A lamentation over the body, the soul, & the life 45

44. A lamentation over God 46
45. A lamentation over God 47
46. A lamentation over God 48
47. A lamentation over God's love 49
48. A lamentation over memory 50
49. A lamentation over mourning 51
50. A lamentation over the river 52

HYMNS

1. A hymn for the river 55
2. A hymn for the day 56
3. A hymn for being pleased 57
4. A hymn for the fingers of God 58
5. A hymn for faith 59
6. A hymn for being swallowed 60
7. A hymn for the flowering tree 61
8. A hymn for God's fullness 62
9. A hymn for my wife 63
10. A hymn for a stranger 64
11. A hymn for the river 65
12. A hymn for hymning 66
13. A hymn for the body of God 67
14. A hymn for stillness 68
15. A hymn for knots 69
16. A hymn for being with God 70
17. A hymn for a good life 71
18. A hymn for the fear 72
19. A hymn for no identity 73
20. A hymn for the leech 74
21. A hymn for the river 75
22. A hymn for wholeness 76
23. A hymn for the doubt 77
24. A hymn for uncertainty 78
25. A hymn for my wife 79
26. A hymn for my parents 80
27. A hymn for my brother 81
28. A hymn for a tree 82
29. A hymn for hymning 83
30. A hymn for humility 84
31. A hymn for silent calm 85
32. A hymn for constant prayer 86

33. A hymn for faith 87
34. A hymn for the eyes... 88
35. A hymn for the ears 89
36. A hymn for skin 90
37. A hymn for the senses 91
38. A hymn for the senses 92
39. A hymn for never rebelling, never conforming 93
40. A hymn for the river.. 94
41. A hymn for death 95
42. A hymn for knowing "God is this!" 96
43. A hymn for no hope or expectation 97
44. A hymn for the body 98
45. A hymn for the river.. 99
46. A hymn for creation.. 100
47. A hymn for the still wheel 101
48. A hymn for every ugliness 102
49. A hymn for God in the rain 103
50. A hymn for the love of God 104

Lamentations

1

A lamentation over a man of God:

Oh God: I am one of your men: I am *a man of God*—so why this: why was I stripped naked before my people (who also suffered this): & why was I blinded & made to dance with a girl, naked, from our town: why were we thrown together for shame: or made to stand atop a pile of bodies: atop a pyramid of dead & still breathing life, life you'd given: & why were one of your symbols (a symbol of your good) carved into my chest: why was a pregnant woman I could only hear shot in her belly & allowed to sob for so long before they shot her too?

Oh God, I am one of your men: I am *a man of God*—& why did they hate this: why with my torn eyes did they beat me & so many others: & why after each strike would they laugh & say *Where is your God?* & why when you gave me my breath back for a moment could I not respond?

2

A lamentation over a community:

Oh God: why were we stripped naked in the cold of those awful days: why were some of us still alive after so many were beaten & killed—why were we left alive only to be marched down a road to die there? Why did men in fine uniforms (& with the ability to speak & to cry & to create) use their abilities to stand or to sit or fix a car or communicate over so many miles—why were these things only used to march us naked down a road to our deaths, while they smoked or sipped coffee, coffee that was so warm?

Oh God, how did we do it? You must have given us the strength to walk the way we did, to see our neighbors as we passed: our neighbors who looked at our uncovered bodies with shame, & yet were in some kind of awe at us.

3

A lamentation over a daughter:

Oh God: I'm not perfect (you know this): & my family was not perfect: we were cruel & frustrated as everyone is. But why did my father have such white hair: why did you give him hair so white & long I knew it when he passed, dead in a pile with others stacked in a wagon?

Oh God, we weren't perfect (you know this): we were only another family. But why were we separated the way we were: & why for a moment was there hope that we would die, at least, together? Why when I got there & waited: & why after waiting so long did that wagon pass?

Oh God, why did you give him such long, white hair? & why was I able to save myself by not reacting: by not crying for my own father for hours—why did you bother giving me the strength to restrain myself when there was nothing to look forward to anymore?

4

A lamentation over a child:

Oh God: I saw my friend from across the road thrown from a window: & I saw when he hit the ground how his face cracked open, my friend's face.

Oh God, they came to our door & our stairs & mother tried to hide me but they shot her: & they took me downstairs: & I saw other friends & other bodies all over the road I used to run down.

Oh God, I tried to run but they took me by my legs & swung me in the air so fast & down my head split before I could feel it.

5

A lamentation over a mother:

Oh God: we hid in the wall: we hid in the wall with others & waited for them to pass: we hid in the wall but my baby wouldn't stop crying: we hid in the wall but my baby's cries would give us away: we hid but would be found by his terrible sobs.

Oh God, I held him so close: oh God, I covered his face with my hands, I held him so close I thought he would dissolve: I thought with his cries & my own he would melt into me so I could bear him again—oh God, I thought you would give me this miracle, to hide my baby back in my belly.

Oh God, but I killed him though. I killed him with the body he came from: the body you gave me: the breasts. & why God did I suffer that only to be found in a day: found & shot & barely buried in your ground? Why did you give me a life at all?

6

A lamentation over many women:

Oh God: give our bodies rest. Our men & our children are killed & we haven't the time to cry or scream for anybody, for anything. & we're stripped naked & killed together: & we scream from the poison & claw at one other & the floor: & we moan with our friends & our sisters & our mothers, all dying with us in a haze of poison on a cold floor.

Oh God: give our bodies rest. Why after this can they not even respect a woman—weren't they born from one? Why do they pry us open to see what we've hidden, & where? Can't we keep one thing if it isn't our life?

Oh God: give our bodies rest. We were thrown dead in a pit with others & are dug up months later: & they burn us & give us ridiculous new life on the wind, in a world sick for death.

7

A lamentation over a man:

Oh God: why couldn't I be a cobbler: why couldn't I be a watchmaker: why couldn't I be a tailor: why couldn't my son or my wife or any of my family have made shoes: or made watches: or made or repaired clothes or done something deemed valuable by these people, to save our lives?

Oh God, I saw five tailors & four cobblers & one watchmaker set aside: I saw them pulled out of line & set aside: & I saw how relieved they looked: & I never hated men more than these, who were pulled out of line: who will fix their uniforms or make them new ones: who will fix their shoes or make them new ones: who will fix their watches or make them new ones.

Oh God, let me at least stain their uniforms to no repair: let me at least stain the bottoms of their shoes when they come to crush my head. Let me at least give them a look to show them what they've done.

8

A lamentation over a man:

Oh God: a man not much taller than me stands with a club as tall as his chest: & he leans on it & nods for me.

Oh God, is this what you made him for: is this what you made me for, this moment? I didn't have any tears for the men before me in line: I only held my head down: I only watched the hose in the corner keep the ground clean of blood.

Oh God, beside me in line were my neighbors, as guards: & around me now in this small square are my neighbors, as spectators: & I'm too hopeless to care that I'm being beaten to death by this man: beaten by my neighbor who's killed twenty already: beaten to the sound of my neighbors who cheer with each strike.

Oh God, I've known love before, yours & others.

9

A lamentation over a man:

Oh God: what is this? To kill a man, yes: shoot him in the head: hang him: kill him—fine. But what is this? & what have we done to deserve it? I've spent days recalling every wrong word: every fit of anger: every willful neglect toward my wife & children & friends—but can that add up to this? For all of us? What has a child ever done that he needs to be nailed to a wall?

Oh God, I am no prophet: I am no perfect man: I am no ideal father—but why must I run in a line of others through a gauntlet of men with rifle-butts & clubs & worse: & why do they strike at us & beat us down: & why do they tear our heads apart & take out our eyes & beat us more when we don't get up?

Oh God, I feel like a pig, pathetic in my own blood, fallen atop some other man: & we mumble what we can to you.

10

A lamentation over an elderly man:
Oh God: this is not your world. Told to leave our luggage, we strip naked in the cold. We've walked far already: from our homes with promises of work: from here to there & finally this place where we give up even our clothes, my neighbors naked all around, I've known them forever.

Oh God, this is not your world: & I'm still surprised when we come to a pit & see our dead: still amazed that we still gasp to see them there. This isn't your world, oh God. This is some other place, where we're told to lie atop the dead: where some just jump in: where we're all shot, naked men & naked children & naked mothers all killed atop the same.

Oh God, this is not your world—because while shot I'm still alive: & I stand in that pit surrounded by my people: & I yell to those you can't have created *Give me another one*, so I can slump & be done.

11

A lamentation over an elderly man:
Oh God: why can't I die? …My beard's never been this so soft: it rests on me, near so many bodies. I'm so old. They've shot me seven times but I can't go—is this you, God? They let me fall with my walking stick: & I've still so much strength that I grasp it: & I remember where I bought it: I remember it in my hands the moment after, as I walked.

Oh God, why can't I die? There's no wind in this pit: there's no sound. Should I be so much trouble to kill? A mother was shot with her child & they fell & never moved.

Oh God, why can't I die? Around my stick my hands are folded: & I feel the fingernails I always bit, & I want to spit & cough, to get up. Life is still so close.

12

A lamentation over a man:

Oh God: did you make running, for this: did you create enthusiasm, for this? When we saw we weren't going anywhere to work we took the money from our pockets & tore it up: & we tore the rings from our fingers & the jewelry from our ears & smashed them in the ground: & we felt strong.

Oh God, but what strength there, to see the pit? We were naked by then, abandoned: we were in a line & suddenly saw—the men & the pit & our line, one by one. Did you invent our legs for this: did you create pushing hands for this, impatience?

Oh God some of us ran to get there quicker—you gave us no hope. We pushed by to be dead, to just be dead. I jumped in alive & waited.

13

A lamentation over a young woman:

Oh God: my mother was on my right, at least: & one sister next to her: & my aunts beside them: & some friends further down: & even some strangers—& we had our backs to them: & we held our arms, at least, all of us naked at the edge of the pit.

Oh God, the sea (perhaps of your creation) wasn't far away, down the hill to the beach. We were close by & didn't look down once we'd seen the bodies & cried aloud: we were close by but didn't look beside one another: we were close by but only clung to familiar hands & arms, to friendly skin. & we all shivered, it was so cold, & stared off at the water. How it came in & went away.

14

A lamentation over a woman:

Oh God: there are men around without weapons: men who have no part in this but are here & who don't understand what they're seeing. & one looks at me: he looks at my nudity & how we all have a hand on the shoulder of the woman ahead of us.

Oh God, they don't understand: they want cries: they want tears: they want rage. I'm done with all that: my family are all dead: I'm not here anymore.

Oh God, I saw one of your men (*a man of God*) dressed all in white: & as he approached the pit I saw him faint at all these things: & I saw him thrown in & shot. If I could only faint. I don't even know how I breathe.

15

A lamentation over a young woman:

Oh God: I never knew how dark the ground was: I never knew how white my skin was: I never knew how much I glowed next to the ground.

Oh God, down there, in the pit dug in the earth, are the white bodies of beautiful women, glaring & golden. Together they are a bloody pearl: together they are a melted sun, one long white body torn apart & stretched through this huge grave. I don't understand people.

Oh God, is this suffering, this last second: am I numb in silence? Oh God, shouldn't I have seen this before, how my own hand & all my people shine on the earth?

16

A lamentation over a man:

Oh God: they brought us into a schoolyard & for fun made us remove horse-dung with our hands: & we moved it from one pile & made another while they laughed—& then with a hose they made us wash.

Oh God, & then others came from over the wall with spades & crowbars & sticks: & they crowded us in that space & swung at us with all those things till we were cut open on the ground—& I saw spectators by the wall, watching.

Oh God, I fainted & thought I was done but I woke to the cold hose-water on my face & gasped & was stunned: & they came to me with more & made sure I was dead.

17

A lamentation over a young woman:

Oh God: we were crowded into this basement & locked here with no bread or water, only men above us with guns. & they would shoot if someone began to talk: & they would shoot if someone moved.

Oh God, there was a well of water down there but we starved: & after a day the air was horrible: & in the night they would come down & steal our things, or they would beat us when we had no more jewelry.

Oh God, I stayed where I was & hoped no light would come to me: no sound—I hoped for only the cold ground. It took a few days to bring my knees up to my chest, & I hugged my own cold body.

18

A lamentation over a young woman:
Oh God: mothers died before their children, & these abandoned things cried & cried. & in the night the men came with flashlights & found what women were still alive: & to a crowd of a dozen of them & the dead mothers & the sobbing babies, the living women were made to take off their clothes & dance.

Oh God, I was one of these. I don't know what joy they found in my starved body. As I danced I only saw a dozen lights on me: & their laughter & cheers came from the dark.

Oh God, but it gave them joy, these men: & they carried me thrashing from that basement to the woods: & they raped me again & again. Oh God what is this gladness that ends with my face broken by a gun, my body cast beside a tree?

19

A lamentation over a daughter, wife, & mother:
Oh God: they stopped raping a woman only when they saw me watching. Weren't *they* watching: weren't her children watching?

Oh God, thirteen houses were burnt with everyone inside: & anyone who escaped was met by them on the lawn, & killed with the street in flames.

Oh God, I snuck out to where I heard my mother was: & I found her atop the other bodies in an awful pit: my poor mother with her face down & body stiff.

Oh God, my husband & son are still gone & I'm looking for them everywhere. Oh God, you've scattered everything.

20

A lamentation over a woman:

Oh God: we were arranged in rows of ten & led away: & it made no sense until it suddenly did & we saw the pit & I began to kiss their boots with the other women—I took off my rings & watch to bribe them.

Oh God, nearby was a row of men: & among them was one of your men (*a man of God*): & he saw us & said *Comfort ye, comfort ye, my people*: but we only moaned more: & that man was only hit with a rifle.

Oh God, then the rows were broken: we were all desperate & some ran ahead. But I sat down: I sat on the ground & waited for a miracle from you to stop this massacre.

21

A lamentation over a witness:

Oh God: the man walked by me upon the road, from fire to fire: the man walked by me upon the destroyed road, from destruction to destruction: the man walked by me upon the road & never saw me, only another stump.

Oh God, he sang as he went & a baby was impaled on his upturned bayonet: & he sang as the baby still cried.

Oh God, he stepped cheerfully as he came, some kind of joy in his face & body for what he & others were doing, his face filthy with blood but his mouth wide & full of some happy song.

22

A lamentation over two men:

Oh God: they were tired perhaps, sick of killing us: oh God, perhaps they just wanted something else to see (they did laugh as they watched us).

Oh God, they took me & a man I knew & told us to beat each other to death: & they said whoever survived would be allowed to live. Oh God, we knew this was a lie: & oh God, neither of us wanted to live (there was no one left) —but we still knocked each other down: we still knocked each other down, I don't know why.

But we were starved: we were tired: we couldn't fight for long & were sick of our bodies & sick of breathing. & they shot me & hanged that man I knew—& oh God, I don't think you saw any of it, were there for any of it, near my shot body behind the building where they all slept.

23

A lamentation over a young man:

Oh God: we knew they were coming next morning: oh God, others prayed but I didn't bother—I didn't want to leave anything for them: I didn't want them to shoot me in the street & then stuff themselves with my food, or drink themselves on my wine.

Oh God, I'd prayed enough before & that last night crammed myself with all I had: neighbors came & we drank & ate: we pretended some celebration & drank till we stumbled to our last sleep & our final morning.

Oh God, but I was clear when they came—I thought I would fall over: I thought I would still be drunk & just stumble to my death. But you cleared my head, God: you couldn't even let me die drunk & stupid on the ground.

24

A lamentation over a community:

Oh God: they put us in the pit without shooting us as we expected: they put us in the pit alive & let us stand there, staring at them. At our feet was a layer of quicklime, & we were all packed together.

Oh God, a truck came after awhile: & they began to fill our pit with water: & the quicklime at our feet began to burn: & our feet began to burn: & we began to burn.

Oh God, the ones who did this to us couldn't take our cries as we boiled: & they went to the piles of our clothes & tore shreds to stuff their ears.

25

A lamentation over a mother:

Oh God: I'm a mother like any mother: I'm a mother like any mother—one child or ten, a mother is a mother.

Oh God, my boy was like any boy: a grown boy or a small boy, only one boy or two or three—a boy is a boy, a child, come from his mother.

Oh God, you saw it, the man took my boy from me & swung him by his feet against a car: & when I cried out he used my own boy's body to hit me in the face.

Oh God, wasn't he precious: am I not precious: were my husband & family not precious? Oh God, aren't we all precious to you anymore?

26

A lamentation over a enslaved man:

Oh God: I am exchanged for dates: I am traded for dates: I am traded for grain—a sack of something on a shelf is the same as my life.

Oh God, there is escape, but into what: into your desert: into your heat: into your distances that only mean hallucination & fever. There was no need to put us in chains, since so few would run to the desert.

Oh God, because when they found me, not even a day out & delirious, they slashed the back of my feet & crushed my manhood with their shoes—& they left me there God, in your desert & your heat.

27

A lamentation over a community:

Oh God: when the rainy season comes let them find us here: when the rainy season comes let them find us by the thousands around dry hollows: when the rainy season comes let them find our skeletons in these same positions, as we searched for water.

Oh God, when the rainy season comes let the falling water remember the sounds of all our screams, & give them back to the ears of those who did this. When the rainy season comes make the rain like flames burn them in the desert they forced us into to die.

Oh God, when the rainy season comes make them insane with fury & thirst: have someone seal them away like they did us & let them die the way we died, digging for water in the desert under your sun.

28

A lamentation over a community:

Oh God: they come & want the rubber from our trees: they come & want the ivory from our elephants: they come & want us to take all these things & give it them, & never pay us but with the whip.

Oh God, when we refuse our hands are cut off: when we refuse our homes are burned down: when we refuse our children are murdered.

Oh God, I saw them force a small boy to cut off a dead man's hand: I saw the boy horrified to do it: but I saw a bag of such hands given to another in charge, & he smiled as if it were food, as it were gold.

29

A lamentation over a hanged man:

Oh God: they say I raped one of their daughters: they say I killed her: & they've put me on this platform to punish me.

Oh God, the father of the girl beats me: oh God, the brother of the girl beats me: oh God, the two of them burn me with irons from my feet & legs to my head: oh God, the two of them put the irons to my eyes: oh God, they put an iron down my throat. Oh God, seeing that I still breathe, oil is poured & I'm put on fire.

Oh God, a crowd of ten thousand was there, beneath my gallows: & they cheered when the noose was put around my neck: & they hollered when I began to burn: & they fought through the rubble after, for my bones.

30

A lamentation over those in mines:

Oh God: it doesn't matter that I'm sick: it doesn't matter that another is maimed: it doesn't matter another is old—oh God, you made us so we would mine.

Oh God, it wouldn't matter if we were women: it wouldn't matter if I were a child: it wouldn't matter if we were anything else at all—oh God, you made us so we would mine.

Oh God, it doesn't matter if we prefer the light: it doesn't matter if we would like to live another way: it doesn't matter that we desire death more than life, or that we hate the darkness of the mines. You made us so we would mine.

31

A lamentation over a slave ship:

Oh God: we've been taken: we've been stolen: we've been put in irons: we're leaking & we're bleeding: oh God, our legs & arms are all swollen, & split.

Oh God, the sky is blue & the water is blue but we're in neither, though we would prefer to swim, to fly.

Oh God, they have their whips: & oh God, on the decks of their ships they make us dance: they make us dance & sing. & we sing so sadly: & they only whip more with for us to *Dance, sing, dance*: & the pools of our sickness covers the deck like some slaughterhouse.

32

A lamentation over a slave ship:
Oh God: in the bottom of their boat we're chained: in the bottom of their boat we're given less room than a corpse in a coffin: in the bottom of their boat we're starved & sickened & swimming in everyone's waste.

Oh God, we can't stand to breathe this: oh God, you didn't make us to breathe. Oh God, down here we breathe quickly & desperately: oh God, down below we breathe like animals.

Oh God, a man comes through now & then: & he takes off his shoes: & we can barely bite at his feet with our teeth.

33

A lamentation over a slave ship:

Oh God: when I refuse to eat they hold my hands & lay me across the windlass: they tie my feet & they whip me.

Oh God, I would have jumped over the side: oh God, I would have jumped to your ocean, but there're nets up for that: & those who've tried are caught: & those who've tried are cut: they're cut & then whipped, for refusing to eat.

Oh God, once three men made it over: once three men made it to the water & two drowned: once three men made it to the water & the only one to live was lifted out & whipped for preferring drowning, or anything, to this life you've given.

34

A lamentation over a slave:

Oh God: the man who owns me needs to be fanned: the man who owns me is warm & when he sleeps, he needs to be fanned. Oh God, the man you've sold me to lies back like some god as I fan him.

Oh God, a woman in the house is loaded with an iron machine on her head: & it locks her mouth—& she cannot eat: & she cannot speak: & she cooks the man his dinner.

Oh God, I'm told the man is sick, the one I fan. His face is red & looks warm: & I'm afraid the clock in the room will wake him: I'm afraid he'll wake & complain: I'm afraid to think anything about him.

35

A lamentation over fathers, husbands, & brothers:
Oh God: the men who own us rape our women: the men who own us rape our daughters, girls not even ten.

Oh God, you gave life to these men so they could rape our wives: you gave life to our girls so they could be raped by these men.

Oh God, our wives gave birth & our daughters came from their mothers so they could be raped by the same men, & saved or helped by none of their own fathers or husbands or brothers.

36

A lamentation over a slave:

Oh God: I was beaten & my bones broken for letting a pot boil over: I was beaten & whipped for burning breakfast toast too much: I was beaten & for fun shoved in a box I barely fit in, & kept there.

Oh God, I tried to get away on a boat but was caught & brought back: I tried to get away but when I was caught the man who owned me—one of your children, who sees you every seventh day—pinned me down by my wrists & ankles: & he poured wax on my back: poured wax all into the wounds he'd already torn there.

Oh God, should I kneel to you?

37

A lamentation over a slave ship:
Oh God: on their ship we didn't want to eat: on their ship we didn't want to live.

Oh God, on their ship they crushed our fingers so our mouths would open: they burned our lips so our mouths would open: they forced food down our open mouths so we would stay alive, for them.

Oh God, we wanted to starve: we wanted to die: we wanted shut our mouths to speech & our eyes to every sight & our ears to every sound: to stop our skin from every touch of dead or living skin, & the drift & sway of their boat on the water forever.

38

A lamentation over a family:

Oh God: they say you allow this: they say you wrote it yourself in your book: they say you said a man could own another if he's a foreigner: you said a man could own a woman if she's a stranger: you said a man could own the children of any foreign couple, could buy & sell them if they were heathens.

Oh God, did you mean me? Am I a man or am I foreigner? I can't be both. Is my wife a woman or a stranger? She can't be both. Are my children actually children, or aren't they?

Oh God, what is a heathen but a man who does what is done to my people? What is a stranger but a people who does these things to another people? What kind of God is it who writes this in his own book?

39

A lamentation over a widow:

Oh God: I believe in you—oh God, I have no family left, so there's only you. I have faith in you: I have faith in your goodness but understand there will always be awful things. But why so many: why all the slaughter I've seen: all the bones broken & the humiliation?

Oh God, I believe in you—oh God, I have no husband left, or home, so there's only you. I have hope in you: I have hope that this will one day end: I pray that this will one day end: I'm on my knees that this will one day end—but it only goes on.

Oh God, I believe in you—oh God, I barely have any life left, so there's only you. I love you. I love you, but do you love me? If I ever hear you insulted I spit & defend you—but where were you when I was raped: when I was beaten: when all around me are murdered or live only in humiliation? How silly I only have you, blind, deaf and dumb as you are.

40

A lamentation over the hands, legs, & heart:

Oh God: these hands are yours: you created them, & merely gave them to me—why do you consent to their destruction? Why do you allow hands that could praise you to be cut off & broken, to be bound?

Oh God, these legs are yours: you created them, & merely gave them to me—why do you consent to their destruction? Why do you allow healthy legs that could praise you & work for goodness to be beaten & broken, to be bound or blown off?

Oh God, this heart is yours: you created it, & merely gave it to me—why do you consent to its destruction? Why do you allow a full heart that only wants to love to be broken? Why do you let it care when you only look on as these things happen?

41

A lamentation over the eyes, ears and skin:

Oh God, these eyes are yours: you created them, & merely gave them to me—why do you consent to their destruction? Why do you allow eyes that could see & love & praise you to only watch more horror?

Oh God, these ears are yours: you created them, & merely gave them to me—why do you consent to their destruction? Why do you allows ears that could hear, that can care, that can enjoy the life you've given—why do you only stuff them with moans & cursing & despair—have you no ears yourself?

Oh God, this skin is yours: you created it, & merely gave it to me—why do you consent to its destruction? Why do you allow skin that can feel & touch & hold, that is capable of great care & compassion & gentleness—why is now the time to touch wounds, to touch burns, to feel beneath my fingers the bodies of those I love?

42

A lamentation over the mind, soul, & life:
Oh God: this mind is yours: you created it, & merely gave it to me—why do you consent to its destruction? Why do you allow a mind you created & gave for so many good things to be crowded with hatred & disgust & hopelessness? What use is a world that is only perceived & experienced this way?

Oh God, this soul is yours: you created it, & merely gave it to me—why do you consent to its destruction? Why is a soul even possible if its presence is so doubtful? What is the use of my burning devotion for you & for every higher thing when prayers are stomped from the mouth?

Oh God, this life is yours: you created it, & merely gave it to me—why do you consent to its destruction? How is life so good when it is only fear: only pride: only arrogance & hatred & weakness turned to violence?

Oh God: spare me any reward when I die: spare me any punishment for these words: spare me all but the ability to rot & forget.

43

A lamentation over the body, the soul, & the life:

Oh God: what use this body, torn by other bodies: what use this body, beaten by other bodies: what use this body, raped & drowned & tortured by other bodies: what use this body, when it & every other only seeks the death of another?

Oh God, what use this soul, torn by doubt: what use this soul, beaten by the senses, the horror of your creation: what use this soul, swarmed by jealousy & sadness & revenge: what use this soul, smothered so easily by every awful impulse?

Oh God, what use this life, terrified to live: what use this life, terrified to die: what use this life, terrified of terror: terrified of itself & all else, defensive, impulsive, brutal to keep the terror away? What use this life, loveless & filled with fear?

44

A lamentation over God:

Oh God: it must pain you: it must hurt you, to see this. Oh God, it hurts when I see a child throw the smallest food to the ground, & squander it—how must it feel to watch the world squander itself: squander you: squander every good thing for terror & arrogance?

Oh God, it must anger you: it must fill you with rage, to see this. Oh God, because I've starved in my life, & when I saw anyone waste food I wanted to strangle them—so how angry you must be, how enraged, every day, to watch all you've formed collapse into competition & jealousy & weakness.

Oh God, it must pain you: it must anger you, to see this. But where is your hand: where is your judgment: where are your tears (your tears I would take!): where is any compassion & generosity: where are your eyes? Don't you see me, dead like garbage in this pit, with the billions?

45

A lamentation over God:

Oh God, I'm going to see if I can go about as you do: I'm going to imagine how you are—& so I'll sit here: & I'll fold my hands: & as the mother is dragged from her home: & as whatever is done to her is done, & as she calls to me for help (since I'm you for the moment) I'm going to sit here, with my hands folded.

Oh God, I'm going to see if I can go about as you do: I'm going to imagine how you are—& so I'll stand here: & I'll cross my legs: & I'll watch as cities full of my faithful are murdered & burned & butchered, & as they call to me for help (since I'm you for the moment) I'm going to stand here, with my legs crossed.

Oh God, do we annoy you? Does the sound of our cries make it hard for you to sleep: does the way we fumble through our lives make you sick at having made us? How can you just stand there?

46

A lamentation over God:

Oh God: tell me what this means: tell me what this puddle means, dirty earth made mud from water runoff or hosed or fallen from your sky or somewhere.

Oh God, tell me what this means: tell me what this puddle means, dirty earth beside a building that used to be here, & parts of it that still are, ash in the ground, families.

Oh God, tell me what this means: tell me what this puddle means, this field, the earth you made, covered in bodies instead of grass, bodies instead of grass, filled with bodies instead of seed, bodies instead of seed, ground that screams & will become silent, screams & will become silent, century to century.

47

A lamentation over God's love:

Oh God: some say you love me: some say your love for me is so great no other love is needed. Some say your love for me is so great the sky could never contain it: so great the earth could never hold it: so great even *great* is too weak a word. Oh God, some people say these silly things.

Oh God, some say you care for me: some say your care for me is so great no other care is needed. Some say your care for me is so great the concern of anyone else is useless: so great that if everyone I loved & cared for died, there would still be you. Oh God, some people say these ridiculous things.

Oh God, some say you are all I need: some say you are so great there is nothing *but* you. Some say you are so great every distraction in the world is useless & passing, & should be abandoned, & that you are the only thing that lasts—& that you will never forget me—that you will never abandon me, my God. Oh God, some people say these awful things.

48

A lamentation over memory:

Oh God: help me forget: help me forget all I've seen & all I've lost: help my mind overlook the old street: the old town: the days that were here in the palm of my hand, my family & my love & my life.

Oh God, help me forget: help me forget all I've seen & all I've felt: help my mind never remember the horror of your world: the lives destroyed for an idea or an old grudge, with perfect righteousness.

Oh God, help me forget: help me forget all I've hoped & imagined I was sure of: help me forget my faith & all the false strength in every lie & every thing. Oh God, turn my head away, turn my head away from you.

49

A lamentation over mourning:

Oh God: let me mourn. Oh God, I'm tired, let me mourn: let me find one corner in your ruined world to sit: to rest: to slow down, to weep, to mourn. Oh God, let me mourn.

Oh God, let me mourn. Let me imagine my mother in my arms: my father in my arms: my wife & children in my arms—let me find one tree in your world to sit under, & imagine their sad bodies in my arms, their eyes still open to you. Please let this stop: please one moment of silence: please one moment of stillness. Oh God, let me mourn.

Oh God, let me mourn. Let me close my eyes & hear no sound: feel no trembling in your earth overhead, no crowds that I dread coming closer in the distance. Let my eyes close & cry for all this shame & hatred & fear. Let me fold my hands to you, dear God, & let me mourn.

50

A lamentation over the river:

Oh God: the sky of your creation is dark with smoke: the sky of your creation is red with fire: the sky of your creation is silent of all life & only filled with the roar of death.

Oh God, the earth of your creation is turned over & destroyed: the earth of your creation is razed: is rubble: the earth of your creation, brick & bone & skin all of the same worth, steel & bone & skin of the same worth, cities & every life useless & wasted, buried in your mess.

Oh God, while your sky may clear: while your earth may come to order, it's only a lie, the worst hope. Your rivers will only ever run blood.

HYMNS

1

A hymn for the river:

Oh God: I came to the river to wash: to see your fish: to dangle my toes in the water—yet I come to the river & you give me visions.

I turn my back from the city to find you: I hear you more clearly near the river & the grass. I turn my back on the city to find you—& you give me visions.

I came to the river for a drink of water, only a sip: I came to the river for a sip of water & some coolness on my hands, some relief for my body & some quiet so I might pray—& there above the grass your visions come to me.

But why this vision: why burning cities & so much noise? I turned my back on the city to see you—but you only show it to me again. Are you in the city? So be it. Whether fire or water from you, I'll drink or burn, better than any other life.

2

A hymn for the day:
Oh God: you aren't the morning or the bed or the sunlight that wakes us: oh God, you aren't the breeze or the bath or the soap or our breakfast: you aren't her lips as she leaves before me—oh God, you aren't my belt or pants or books or the water I wet my hair with. You aren't my shoes or the ground they touch or the people or cars that pass before I can cross: you aren't work or any other thing taken up out of fear or want or need or necessity.

Oh God, you cannot be all of these things. You can't squeeze yourself into a soap bubble: or between two mouths: or into a belt-loop. You can't lie in the knot of my shoes: or simultaneously in my suddenly combed hair & the brush, can you?

Oh God, you can't be in every customer who rushes, never thinking of you. Yet I think if you aren't between my stepping feet & the stepped-on ground, where are you? Where are you if not in the wind: if not everywhere?

3

A hymn for being pleased:

Oh God: who am I to ask what you are or aren't? Who am I to do anything but wonder: who am I to be anything but pleased? If you are merely a metaphor I am pleased: if you have a thousand names in as many tongues I am pleased. (Water, after all, is called a thousand things in as many tongues—& why shouldn't you be as lucky?) & if you're portrayed a million ways in paint or stone: called on a million ways in words & cries & rituals—let me only be pleased.

Let others argue over which name is closest: which gestures most pure: which prayers most efficacious—let me only be pleased. Let others use proof to support you: & others violence: & others arrogance: & let others not believe at all—but let me only be pleased. Let the rest do what they must & call you what they can to sleep well— & let me only be pleased.

4

A hymn for the fingers of God:

Oh God: when I say you are everywhere I want you to know what I mean: I want you to know how I see. I don't mean I will ever worship or call upon or pray to the rhythm of my steps on the sidewalk: or the calls of people from car-windows: or the decency of a man I meet whose wife has just died: or the music of whoever in my ears.

I will never depend on the grass or the pillow to my face or a thunderstorm at midnight—but I will smile to always see you, everywhere: inside of & to the left of me: inside of & to the right of me: & above me & below me. Like the happiness of a husband for his wife's body I will never forget to gaze upon your entirety—yet at times I will have to smile, even, at the sight of your fingers, dear God.

5

A hymn for faith:

Oh God: don't give me comfort & don't give me peace: don't give me certainty or any security. Give them if it is your will, but I won't miss them if you don't: I won't miss the attention of the rich or the well-known: I won't demand justice from anyone if they insult me: I won't cry to you if I never have enough money: & I won't even wonder at the innocent millions who suffer. Only others demand these: only others demand answers or signs in return for faith: only others who can't sleep soundly unless your scales are ready.

Faith is enough: to always be ignited by you is enough: to feel every corner of me consumed by your love is enough. Oh God: please don't be something so human as a judge: please only be something as divine as God: please only be revelation.

6

A hymn for being swallowed:

Oh God: never let me forget some must see you in stone, a statue standing there, or a roof or dome done in the image of you: never let me forget some must find you in words, in colored drops of you on paper that spell your billion names: never let me forget so many come nearer you with only beads & their trailing fingers & their closed eyes: never let me forget some come into you with not even these, only a posture & something inside.

Oh God, never let me forget all these circles round that spiral into you: never let me find arrogance in one or condemnation in another, for these don't come from you.

Oh God, let me only find those things that lead to you: let me watch you consume every opposite: let me see you take up every road in a great wind: let me watch as you swallow even the sea.

7

A hymn for the flowering tree:
Oh God: I realized you are like the flowering tree outside our window: it's always there behind the drapes & the shears: behind the window & the screen & our cats watching—& across an always-dirty alley to someone's backyard & even behind a fence.

It's always there but we forget until the window is open & a wind picks up & we're on the bed to smell it—& then we do smell it, what's always been there: as if we just found it again.

8

A hymn for God's fullness:

Oh God: you are full: so I am full. You are full: so my wife is full. You are full: so my family is full. You are full: so we all are full. May you always be full: may we always be full: may you never empty & may we all never empty.

May all seen & heard be covered by you, God: may all with a scent or a touch be covered by you, God: may all that's tasted or intended or considered or remembered or created only in the heart or mind be filled & covered & gilded over & made supreme & permanent by you, dear God.

May your grace be as a glass of water at noon: & may every moment be as unbearable as the warmest sun of the worst noon if every moment we may expect your grace beneath us: your grace all over us: your grace filling us & fulfilling us: your grace like water down our throats & over every limb that needs you so.

9

A hymn for my wife:

Oh God: as I die I see you are bright & bodiless: & as I burn after I'm gone (or slowly brush away beneath ground instead) may I be the same: may my bones shine bright in the fire or bright in the ground darkness.

But make my final brightness in you: make me bright in your presence: give me light from your side & give me gold from your brow: let me stare with perfect eyes upon a vision I cannot imagine even now, as I die.

& give my wife this glow: give my wife this light: let me haunt her with this shining: let me merge with you but stay with her as well (I know only you can allow this): & let all I was become one part ash in your palm & another part heart, still beating, in her body. Oh God let me whisper to her now & then *Remember: remember all we have done!*

10

A hymn for a stranger:

Oh God: how is it I falter when all you are is joy? Sometimes you seem far away & I say of others *God isn't who he worships*—but did you give me my head only so I would be this stupid?

Other times you're so near: & you show me the birds near the pier: & you show me the birds near the park: & when I run out of bread I want to say to each one *Stay here, Lord, while I get more.*

But why when a stranger stops me with some words do I try to mutter *Wait another moment, God, while I think of something to say*: & why does nothing come: why can't I talk to this person like I talk to you: why can't I see you there, in another man's eyes, & instead want to close my own & pray in quiet fear?

11

A hymn for the river:
Oh God: I was a child by the river when I first saw you: a child by the great waters when I heard the voice of your speech & the noise of your host (all those names & masks) when they let down their wings by the riverside & you appeared as you are, one. & I sat where you stood, astonished, for days: & you taught me to care & not to care: you taught me to sit still. You told me to drink carefully: you said to eat carefully: you said to speak little, but carefully.

& being only a child you made me measure the length of the river where you appeared: & an equal length back into the land where you appeared: & you told me this square was a holy place. & being only a child you told me to remember those measurements: & you said to drop them anywhere in the world: you said any square of space, larger or smaller, was just as holy: & you assured me & said *There are other children: there are further places: & this isn't the only river.*

12

A hymn for hymning:
Oh God: I don't ever want to raise my head to you & cry: I don't want to imagine I can grab the dirt of your earth & toss it at you in anger: I don't want to tear my clothes or curse because of something I assume you've done.

I don't want what the world wants: I don't want their recognition or their power or the things that keep them smiling so weakly.

Keep bitterness at bay: keep jealousy outside: keep distraction in another corner—keep me from their arguments: keep me from their opinions: keep me from ever defending anything, even you: ever explaining even one word: ever imagining I can do anything but wonder this way.

Keep me from entering the fray of babblers whose best music is their own voice: whose best distractions are others' voices & their own, endlessly: babblers who would say nothing if they weren't noticed. I don't want another's envy: I don't want another's eyes: I only want to hymn.

13

A hymn for the body of God:
Oh God: if as it's said you don't have a body, whose hand do I feel every day: if you don't have ears, how do you hear me: if you can't speak, what do I hear when I'm sure it's you?

Oh God, if as it's said you don't have a body, who did I see near the river as a child: who do I see near the river even now: & who do I see everyday gliding between strangers & inside them?

If as it's said you don't have a body, oh God, who do I taste when I take your food: & who do I smell when the food is being cooked: or when the candles are lit: or when you take the dead with you & leave incense behind?

14

A hymn for stillness:

Oh God: I understand I'm apart from others: I understand I & the rest are like two birds on a branch: I understand others are the bird who flies & eats & makes small music for all to hear—& I understand I'm the one who doesn't fly & doesn't eat & makes no music: I understand I'm the bird who only watches.

But it's hard to watch! How easily watching becomes criticism: how easily observing becomes disapproval: how easily what I was meant to do becomes poisoned with jealousy: bitter with restlessness: distracted by color & motion & all things that only amuse.

Help me God to watch & be silent: help me God to watch & be still: help me God to watch & not move an inch: not move even a thought.

15

A hymn for knots:

Oh God: without you my heart is a knot, all is a knot: my feet are knots so I can't walk: my hands are knots so I drop everything: my eyes are knots so everything blurs, everything is painful, everything is criticized—& my stomach & my throat & my mouth are all knots, & I can eat but can't enjoy any of it, & am always hungry & never full.

& my ears are knots, awful knots where everything is heard but nothing discerned: where everything is heard but it's all a piercing hum: where everything is heard but it all stings—& I can't sleep but can hardly roll on one side or another, all night long.

But with you, oh God, my heart is loose & filled: & I can walk: I can hold to things & pass them on: I can see & concentrate & only praise: & I can eat & am filled & feel you all through me. & I can hear—what can't I hear when you are with me?

16

A hymn for being with God:

Oh God: apart from you I am a river: & with you I disappear into your sea. Apart from you I am only one breath blowing: & with you I enter into the wind. Apart from you I'm lonesome, loveless, unknown: & with you I'm one with my wife, forever.

Apart from you I'm a small flame lit in a tiny room struck with a feeble match-stroke: & with you I'm the roaring generous engulfing brightness of the sun. Apart from you I'm a dark corner, a dark closet, a dark edge of an opened door: & with you I am the darkness of beautiful night, stars & calls & all of life in the air.

Apart from you I'm a tree: & with you I'm a forest. Apart from you I'm defending some square of ground from all comers, suspicious on all sides: & with you I'm all the earth. Apart from you I'm only parts, I'm only an eye or a hand or an ear, only a mouth or a nose, a disconnected body—& with you I see & feel & hear: with you I taste & speak & smell: with you I am alive.

17

A hymn for a good life:
Oh God: give me whatever life you want, short or long doesn't matter: give me whatever life you want, success or failure doesn't matter: give me whatever life you want, rich or poor doesn't matter: give me whatever life you want, filled or hungry doesn't matter: give me whatever life you want, strong body or perpetually sick doesn't matter: give me whatever life you want—only take fear away as you give it: take jealousy away as you give it: take envy away as you give it: & leave me only what I need to praise you as you go: leave me only good things in my ears as you go: leave me only good things from my mouth as you go: as you stay immediately here.

Oh God give me whatever life you want: take all that so many others might want & only leave me a table & a room where I might say *This food has been prepared for you, oh God.*

18

A hymn for the fear:

Oh God: but I'm afraid: afraid of loss: afraid of losing you: or my wife: afraid of the looks of others: afraid of others' words: afraid of how I appear.

How can I have faith in you but still be afraid? How can I believe yet feel such unbelief? How can I avoid so much yet still feel ashamed when faced with it? How can I still be ashamed of silence: ashamed of obscurity: ashamed of the same shirts & a few pair of pants: ashamed of my hair or eyes or every other useless clod of appearance—how after all you've shown me can I still be ashamed of you?

How can I still wish for eloquence & charm & personality when you show me moment after moment how silence is crystal: anonymity is the sun: & humility is the greatest of things—& sympathy even more?

19

A hymn for no identity:

Oh God: while I've always tried to use words: while I may have come to love the early evening rather than the day: while the food I love is this & not that—don't let me be any of these more than I am you.

Oh God, while this is the skin you've given me: while I may have been born here instead of there: while my near-blind eyes have always identified me—don't let me be any of these more than I am you.

Oh God, while this is the name you've given me: while these are the years you've give me life: while these are the things you've given me the grace to see or know or do, none of these are as real as you.

20

A hymn for the leech:

Oh God: you are the sound that follows me as I walk: you are the sound that never lags behind as I run: you are the sound of praise in my body: you are the silence when I stop.

Oh God, when you appear it's like when my wife holds me: when I don't feel or see a thing: when I don't taste or smell a thing: when I don't hear a thing & there's nothing in my head except how inseparable we are: how one we were made.

Oh God, today I watched a leech make its way from one blade of grass to another: I watched it slowly move from one blade of grass to another. Oh God, I think I'm like that leech, going so slowly & with a distance to go, but overjoyed to have made it to another blade: overjoyed when I realize you are each blade anyhow: overjoyed this is what I was always meant to do.

21

A hymn for the river:

Oh God: you appeared by the river again: & the water was no longer water: it was still blue & fell through my fingers & was still cold to my feet—but it wasn't water. It had a new aspect: it became you—& the water was transformed: & the forest was transformed: & the fields around were transformed: & the city I cannot understand was transformed.

& I tried to look up but my eyes were transformed: my eyelids & all I saw were transformed—there was nothing that wasn't transformed.

& I saw a manner of life where you were always revealed: where water replenishes but is never consumed: where fire burns but never ends: where wind blows endlessly & never ceases cooling the sweat on my brow: & where the earth itself is unused yet forever gives, to no end.

Is this what you meant me to see, your ten thousand & many & endless ways: your face in all directions, unterrifying & all good?

22

A hymn for wholeness:

Oh God: is this how I'm supposed to feel? I'm so close to you my body doesn't seem to have *parts* anymore: I'm so close to you I wonder how I taste except by tasting: how I see except by seeing: how I hear except by hearing: how I can touch anything except by touching: how I can smell some scent except by simply smelling: my mouth or eyes or ears or fingers or nose aren't really doing this.

I'm not made of parts: I'm made of you, whole: & even to say I taste *something* is only a separateness that isn't there. Oh God, there's nothing for me to do: there's nothing to happen to me: there's nothing except being you.

23

A hymn for the doubt:

Oh God: some days I'm small: some days I'm nothing & feel you're so far away. Some days I'm lazy or easily angered or I spend all day looking only to criticize.

Oh God, some days I'm afraid: some days I can't say a word to my wife or anyone else: some days I'm sure my prayers are ugly & useless & I'm sure only of the empty burning that comes from idle arguments about you.

Oh God, some days I'm sure everything is death: some days all I see is the skin the snake's left on the ground, not the new one slithering away. Oh God, some days all I see is the huge fire nearly extinguished—& some days it's impossible to see the tiny coal, still red & able to reignite the whole.

Oh God, some days I feel something that isn't even pain: some days I feel something worse than sadness: some days I only feel this useless pity & torpor toward all you have made: some days I can only cry at how empty & unjust you are.

& thank you God for not making this every day.

24

A hymn for uncertainty:

Oh God: please don't keep pain from me: please don't let me conquer doubt: please God never let my faith in you become a certainty.

Please God never let me forget no matter how close to you I come, I'm still alive on your earth: I'm still alive in a place where I shouldn't ever expect justice: expect fairness or decency: shouldn't ever expect anything but what I usually find, hurry & selfishness & worry without end, & ambitions to more misery.

It's true I can be miserable: but at least I'm miserable in you: at least my misery is saved by you: at least my misery is lit by your love, & every ambition of the hands or the eyes is a pile of sand washed away by your reality.

I couldn't stand misery dependent upon others: I couldn't enjoy success dependent upon others: but I will take both & more from you.

25

A hymn for my wife:

Oh God: thank you for my wife: thank you for our love: thank you for the first glimmer of things as I shouted her name when she first appeared on my stoop. Thank you for those first evenings of only words & those subsequent evenings of all else & every impulse you placed inside to show what you meant. Oh God, you didn't force us together: you didn't will us together by some fate—oh God, these things are what humans, or movies, pretend to do. You merely showed us to each other: you merely let us listen: you merely said *Here you are: isn't this what you've been asking for?*

26

A hymn for my parents:

Oh God: thank you for my mother & father: thank you for the seed & center I came from. Thank you for the house I first knew you in: thank you for my room where a picture of you hung always on the wall. Thank you for the window overlooking the street where I first experienced the difference in evening winds: of night sounds without sources: of calls & snatches of talk & sudden bursts of light that subsided in a moment—all these small shadows & hints, for when you came to me full by the river.

Thank you for my mother & father who assured me you could be spoken to: thank you for the immediate reality of their love that allowed you to settle perfectly upon me: that was first to show me the importance of the quiet & the small & the unnoticed, nevermind whatever world remained elsewhere.

27

A hymn for my brother:

Oh God: thank you for my brother. When I first went off he saw where I was going & gave me a small gift & looked at me as if I'd lost my head. But he still gave a small gift: he still shook my hand & hugged me & said some small words. & every time I've gone off since he celebrates with me—the first we were with his friends, but this last we were alone, the two of us at a table the night before I was married. Thank you for him, God: thank you for a kind of goodness it's hard to find in many others I know. & thank you for giving him the same seed as me—because while he is more in the world he still told me *It's best not to be noticed.*

28

A hymn for a tree:

Oh God: like a tree whose branches will always grow after being cut, no criticism or neglect will ever harm you. People want to wonder why you didn't make us like trees, why you didn't give us the hope of losing an arm or worse & growing another—but this is only the excuse of those who know they've wasted their time: who haven't realized that the smallest second turned to you makes up for forever: who would like to reduce you to a diagram: to the God of their infancy: to conform to the banal regularity of their daily schedule: or not exist at all.

It's as if they came upon a tree they never planted & demanded it be another tree entirely. Yet even their actions are washed away by your own earth, always in witness. Your earth is your own best defense: & they would rather rearrange it than realize this.

29

A hymn for hymning:

Oh God: why is it so hard to hymn to you sometimes? Why are the words impossible: why do they make no sense or not come at all? & when they do—why do I worry about them so much? Why do I wonder if I've compared you to enough things: if I've described enough of your everything to give you real praise? & do I praise you enough here: are these too much about me—& even if I praise you with a thousand more is this what you really want: is rearranging words what I was meant to do? Is it enough to make these sound as good as I can— does this actually *praise* you, this rearranging, or is it something I should give up? Should I just think these things without ever writing them: does writing them tear apart the one that I am in you, into the three of you & me & what this all means in words?

30

A hymn for humility:

Oh God: help me be humble: help humility be endless: help the greatest humility come by becoming you: help me have nothing & want nothing & need nothing by becoming you: help there be nothing of me since there's only you: help me come to you that closely, & let that coming be endless.

31

A hymn for silent calm:

Oh God: help me never compare—since there is no comparison with you: help me never need admiration—since yours is all: help me never display myself or try to prove anything—since you are everywhere visible & are your own proof. Help me never care what another thinks—since thoughts of me or anyone else are ridiculous when they could instead be thoughts of you. Help me be as simple & content as you: so simple no defense is needed: so content all argument is quiet: so satisfied every sound is swept up & annihilated by your calm.

32

A hymn for constant prayer:

Oh God: every time I start to argue, let me pray to you instead: every time I start to wonder aloud about some rumor, let me pray to you instead.

Oh God, every time my mind starts to criticize: every time my head wants to fill the necessary silence with waste & distraction & all the flashing lights of every dumb & easy diversion—let me pray to you instead.

Every time I think I'm bored: every time I dwell on something I shouldn't & end up disgusted: every time I begin to think or obsess over the million things that aren't you—let me pray to you instead: let me forget those things that only take & lull & entertain. Let there be no end of my prayers to you.

33

A hymn for faith:

Oh God: how wonderful you are: how perfect: how you make yourself known through all things—so I can't say I must be poor to find you: or rich: or ugly: or beautiful: or living here, or there: or saying those words, or these.

Oh God, how I love it when it rains, since this is how you are: the murderer gets just as soaked as your saint: & when the sun comes out everyone is dried.

Thank you again, God, for leaving judgment & justice, & some obvious line or punishment or reward or will, up to the humans who need this. Thank you for making faith paramount. Thank you for making virtues that your creation cannot apprehend—silence, solitude, anonymity—one of the clearest paths to your side.

34

A hymn for the eyes:

Oh God: what does it mean that I can see a million things in a day or a lifetime: that I can look on a million faces of a thousand colors: that I can see photos or stand at the foot of every mountain: that I can step with my feet on the earth of every country: that I can look on a map & say *I've been there,* or *I know what that place is called*—what does it mean that I can experience every color & every shape & every size by simply living in this time instead of another? What do these possibilities mean, to you? What do these choices mean if only seen vacantly: if only seen as *possible?*

Oh God, so long as they don't stay lit, these are only flashing lights: & these words have described nothing.

35

A hymn for the ears:

Oh God: what does it mean that I can easily hear every language: or even learn a half-dozen—what does it mean that I can hear instantaneous news from a thousand mouths about events four thousand miles away? What does it mean to only hear things because they can be expressed: to only hear words because they can be said: to be interested in words only because they come from somewhere else & not next door? What do these possibilities mean, to you? What do these choices mean if only seen vacantly: if only seen as *possible*?

Oh God, so long as they don't stay lit, these are only flashing lights: & these words have described nothing.

36

A hymn for skin:

Oh God: what does it mean that if I look long enough I can touch a new body every night, or day: what does it mean that at lunch or dinner or anytime I can find any food: or can walk down any street & come upon any scent & simply experience it—what is the value of consuming experience for its own sake: what is the importance of anything that's done simply because it *can* be? Oh God, distraction is the absence of substance, isn't it: & anything is only a distraction when it's only some choice: only some possibility.

Oh God, so long as they don't stay lit, these are only flashing lights: & these words have described nothing.

37

A hymn for the senses:

Oh God: what does it mean that between waking & sleeping I can read a million words: can find a dozen screens where thousands of words are waiting to be read: where cars or buses or trains or every newspaper-stand or store-window are filled with words that tell me to do something: to want something: to need something: words that assure me I'm incomplete without something: words that want to frighten everyone into envying those who've already obeyed them: words that'll just be different words in a day or a month or a year: words built not on wisdom but cheap perpetual change, perpetually cheap & constantly fluctuating efficiency: words that use a blip or phrase to sum up a person or entire country, an entire point in time: words so cheap even those who write them are unsure they mean anything at all. Oh God, what do these things mean to you: & what should they mean to me, with your visions & your words always at hand?

Oh God, so long as they don't stay lit, these are only flashing lights: & these words have described nothing.

38

A hymn for the senses:

Oh God: hold my senses in your million hands: help me to see & not to see: help me to taste & not to taste: help me to smell & not to smell: help me to feel & not to feel: help me to hear & not to hear.

Oh God, help only those things that bring you close: help me not to ignore but to not even notice the billion things that bombard us all day to day.

Help me not become agitated by the world: help me not hate it: help me only to wander through it decently: quietly: help me find my way around those who do hate it: who are indecent: who are loud: who only want speed & the only immortality—immediate recognition—they can comprehend.

Oh God, hold my senses in your million hands: & quiet them till the only evidence of me having ever lived are a thousand people in the future hymning these same thoughts to you.

39

A hymn for never rebelling, never conforming:

Oh God: why should I ever rebel: why should I ever react: why should I ever dismiss or support: why should I ever codify or dogmatize? Why should I ever think a thought by wondering how novel it is compared to the past: or how gladly it dismisses the doldrums of today for the wisdom of awhile ago: or how much it will upset this person, or that?

Oh God, why should anything I ever do be dictated by its possible reception: why should anything I ever do be muddied by my own selfishness: or by bizarre notions of the world's knowledge, & how I'm a part of some tradition?

Oh God, what is the use of all this thought if it's only over-thought: what's the use of all this knowledge if it only leads to more knowledge & more identities & never a stop & never one moment of confident silence?

Oh God, to what use are these mazes when you yourself sit, untroubled & easily found, in the folded flame of my hands?

40

A hymn for the river:

Oh God: by the river today you planted a tree on my tongue & it grew so quickly I nearly choked—but by the time it got that big I was gone anyway. As it burst out my mouth my head split clean & the rest of me wriggled as it was filled with roots: & these burst from my hands & toes, my elbows & my knees.

& then I seemed to swing upside down & was a tree with roots in the sky: & I floated above our beloved river water: & all the branches that used to be my body dangled there & sipped what water they could.

& you sent so many of the dead to me: & they became leaves there: & each of those leaves held words as well, not only souls: & all about me were dead memories still alive & their gratitude to you: & all about me were voices of the dead & of words.

& look! There! Someone down by the river: & how he jumps to me to grab my branches hanging down: & how happy I am for the fruit you've made me, dear God.

41

A hymn for death:

Oh God: I don't mind dying: I don't want to be saved from it: I don't want to conquer it or have you conquer it for me. I'm not afraid of it. If you are at its end I'll be full: if you aren't & there's nothing I'll have had my fill while alive, & with these words, & with you.

I would rather pray to you: or thank you: or sit still somewhere & see you all around & smile, than whine about any fear of death.

Listen to my fears about life, please: & accept my fears about whether I'm living the life you've given me: & take my fears about living on the earth you made: & receive my fears about my wife & whether I'm good for her—but please forget all my fears about death.

Once dead I'll pray to you about it: I'll pray to you about that other world when I'm there, or will address you directly. Yet even there I won't be afraid.

42

A hymn for knowing "God is this!":
Oh God: I can't say you're only in one place. If you're in the sky the birds have you first: if in the earth all of nature has you first—& I'm only doing my best to walk on you. If you're in one specific person: or one specific building: or hidden somehow in the order of one set of words, & these only—someone will always be closer to you than the rest.

If anything you're present to all equally & at all times—if they'll only see you. You're inside of me: you're outside of me: you have no body yet live & see & hear & make sound: you have no body yet are covered in a million mouths everywhere: & a million ears—& everything I see are your hands.

I used to point to all things & say *God's not this, not this*—yet now I see those same things & put my ear to them & hold them up & yell *God is this! God is this!* You stand behind & ahead of all people—yet have no legs: you have no ears yet you hear my words: you have no mouth—yet I hear you as the sun rises.

43

A hymn for no hope or expectation:
Oh God: thank you for teaching me never to look forward: thank you for telling me never to expect: thank you for whispering that whatever I wait for is already behind me.

I see the men you mean all day long: I see in their heads a thousand thoughts & a thousand plans for their money & their time: for themselves & their families: for their futures & their futures—& yet in the night, oh God, while these thoughts are even still running on, these thoughts never end, or they finally die.

Oh God, because of you I don't desire a thing that requires hope: I don't want a thing that takes my attention from your face before me.

Oh God, why should I look forward to your listening ears when I only have to open my mouth: why should I look forward to my wife when she is always beside me?

44

A hymn for the body:
Oh God: why should I hate my body: why should I detest my appetites: why should I loathe my desires: why should I be afraid of aging or death or of anything you've given? & why would you give me this body or this earth if you only meant me to reject them?

Oh God, my soul isn't enough, is it: & it isn't enough either to do away with my body, is it? Sometimes I see you most clearly: sometimes I think I've become as you are: sometimes this happens most deeply when I drink a glass of water: or when my muscles sing & ache for all they've done.

Oh God, you can't mean that we should pluck out our eyes & take a knife to our ears: that we should starve ourselves & stuff our noses so they no longer smell a thing: you can't mean we should somehow float in air & no longer feel anything with the skin you've given. (No, since even then we would feel your wind & rain & heat— & how could the touch of your spirit be sin?) Oh God, you can't have meant that. Those are things people have made for themselves—these things aren't you.

45

A hymn for the river:

Oh God: I don't go to the river to see a rich man & all his money: I don't go to the river to see people looking in their mirrors: I don't go to find people with headphones: I don't go to find preoccupation with a thousand other things: oh God, I don't go to the river to ask for food or want anything or demand something in exchange for something else.

I don't go to the river to barter & receive & experience only in some spirit of begrudging trade: I don't go to the river the way we tolerate people as we go through the day. (I don't "tolerate" the grass because it gets me to the river: I don't tolerate the grass at all: I love it.)

I go to the river to find you: to find a rooftop to shout what I see—I go to the river to experience all things like this.

46

A hymn for creation:

Oh God: just as you created the world down to the hairs on my head, so you've allowed us to create the world as well. It's quiet as you've made it: & it sits there: & it goes on & on with life & death. But any beauty I see comes from me seeing it: any beauty I see comes from me hearing it, or tasting it: any beauty I see comes from my touch or smell of it. & anything ugly comes from inside: anything evil is created by me: anything impure comes from the eyes that've made it impure in my sight.

The same stone: the same sky: the same walk on different mornings: the same meal for two people: a kiss, & then a second one—the meaning of each of these is created from inside, & nowhere else.

Oh God, another child could've seen you at the river that day, & run: or an adult bitter about how they've created their lives—he could have seen you & only blasted anger. But I knew who you were: I saw what you were offering: I allow my visions of you as much as you give them.

47

A hymn for the still wheel:

Oh God: what's left after I stop criticizing? What's left after the end of judgment: what's left when I go out & see someone or something & no longer compare: no longer take it in & spit it out with some commentary?

What's left when all I do is watch? What remains when all I do is see: is listen: is attempt to understand? What lingers when the world is quiet: when to observe something no longer means to sneer to another about it: when disparagement & analysis & ridicule & envy & derision drop off? What happens in that silence?

What's left when I walk your world without these props that hold me down? What's left when the mouths of perpetual & professional babblers are shut?

Oh God, what's left when the wheels stop turning & in the previously blurry hub your face appears, clear as my own reflection?

48

A hymn for every ugliness:
Oh God: don't turn my head away: don't let me turn away from every ugliness: don't let me deny cruelty or suffering (in reality I probably haven't suffered at all).

Oh God: let me see all the spite the world is stuffed with: let me listen to all its envy: let me watch all its violence. Don't let me look away from all the sad arrogance around: all the frightened arrogance: all the fear. Don't let me forget love defeats fear: love casts fear away & fills it up & all fear is forgotten. Never let me ever deny the reality of stupid aggression: & stupidity: & selfishness: don't let me ever deny it every time someone is underestimated: is diminished: is assumed cheap or filthy because of some deep fear: some deep empty space where you've never been allowed: or where some easier version of you has been given a place to live.

Oh God, don't ever let me forget murder: never let me forget the murderer or the murdered: don't let me close the window when they come as a horrible noise outside: don't let me forget their faces: don't let me forget this struggle.

49

A hymn for God in the rain:

Oh God: as it rained today I saw you in how the people acted: I saw how those with umbrellas or only newspapers to cover themselves, or even just their jackets pulled over their heads—I saw how they all ran for whatever doors they could find: I saw huddled groups everywhere just inside whatever buildings or businesses: I saw how they met with other people as wet as them & joked with each other about the rain you sent on them.

Oh God, I think you're like those small spaces where they all ran to be dry: I think all my time anymore is spent running towards a place where I'm sure you are: a place I can quietly see you without getting drenched by every distraction.

But as you know I like the rain: so today I didn't run anywhere: I felt you in the rain & didn't mind getting wet: & I heard your voice in the thunder & sat on the sidewalk to listen: & I let waterfalls of you fall all around me.

50

A hymn for the love of God:

Oh God: do you know my joy in loving you? Do you know the joy of my love with you as its object & end? Do you know the joy of my joy you give me & I give back: do you know the joy of a love so complete it can be separated & given out yet is never diminished & is always complete? Do you know the joy & thanks of my love for the refuge & haven you are: for the simple recognition that "this" may last for five moments, while you last forever?

Oh God, do you know the joy your visions give me, as I walk the street? It must be strange since you have no God to ask these questions—there is no one higher for you to be happy with: you are your own height & depth.

& so: can you imagine the joy of being so close to another so great: do you know the joy I feel at the river when the water begins to stir & I know you are near?

www.ingramcontent.com/pod-product-compliance
Lightning Source LLC
Chambersburg PA
CBHW051953290426
44110CB00015B/2217